Preventing and Managing Conflict in Schools

Neil H. Katz
John W. Lawyer

CORWIN PRESS, INC.
A Sage Publications Company
Thousand Oaks, California

For information address:

Corwin Press, Inc.
A Sage Publications Company
2455 Teller Road
Thousand Oaks, California 91320

SAGE Publications Ltd.
6 Bonhill Street
London EC2A 4PU
United Kingdom

SAGE Publications India Pvt. Ltd.
M-32 Market
Greater Kailash I
New Delhi 110 048 India

Printed in the United States of America

Library of Congress Cataloging-in-Publication Data

Katz, Neil H.
    Preventing and managing conflict in schools / Neil H. Katz, John
W. Lawyer.
        p.   cm. — (Roadmaps to success)
    Includes bibliographical references (pp. 71-72).
    ISBN 0-8039-6146-4
    1. School management and organization—United States. 2. Conflict
management—United States.   I. Lawyer, John W.   II. Title.
III. Series.
LB2866.K277   1994
371.2'01—dc20   94-21624

94 95 96 97 98 10 9 8 7 6 5 4 3 2 1

Corwin Press Production Editor: Marie Louise Penchoen

Contents

Foreword

This book is the third volume in a three-book series that deals with conflict prevention, management, and resolution. Each volume is a stand-alone work; together, they provide teachers and administrators with the knowledge and skills needed to effectively deal with conflict situations in schools.

Conflict Resolution: Building Bridges explores the nature of conflict and its principal sources. *Resolving Conflict Successfully: Needed Knowledge and Skills*, the second volume, presents the core skills essential for managing conflict and negotiating differences.

This volume, *Preventing and Managing Conflict in Schools*, discusses the various means of conflict prevention through effective human interaction: (a) immediacy, (b) agreement setting and management, (c) facilitation, and (d) mediation. It stresses prevention and management of conflict and emphasizes the important role of the facilitator in the conflict resolution process.

All three books are invaluable guides for understanding, learning about, and using conflict prevention, management, and resolution skills.

JERRY J. HERMAN
JANICE L. HERMAN
Series Co-Editors

About the Authors

Neil H. Katz is committed to self-actualization, nonviolence, and participative decision making as a way to influence change among individuals and in organizations and society. His primary interest is facilitating interactive learning and skill development about conflict and its resolution.

Katz serves in a leadership capacity in five different conflict resolution programs in the Maxwell School of Citizenship and Public Affairs at Syracuse University. He is the Director of the Program in Nonviolent Conflict and Change, Director of the Annual Summer Institute on Creative Conflict Resolution, Director of the University Conflict Resolution Consulting Group, Faculty Supervisor of the Campus Mediation Center, and Associate Director of the Program on the Analysis and Resolution of Conflicts.

Katz is a Danforth Teaching Fellow, a process consultant, a mediator, a facilitator, and a trainer in conflict resolution and negotiation skills. His clients include organizations in education, ministry, government, and education. Among his educational clients are the Danforth Foundation, the New York State Council of Superintendents, the New Jersey Department of Education, the U. S. National Science Foundation, the St. Louis Principal's Association, and numerous school systems in New York State and around the country.

Before receiving his doctorate and becoming a college professor, he taught junior high school.

Katz is the author or co-author of over 20 book chapters and articles on conflict resolution and nonviolence and co-author (with Jack Lawyer) of three highly acclaimed workbooks, *Communication Skills for Ministry, Communication and Conflict Resolution Skills*, and *Communication and Conflict Management Skills*.

John W. Lawyer enjoys difference and change. He values himself as a choice maker and creator of processes and models that enable people to become lifelong learners. His primary interest is enabling others to build trusting environments, learn from their experience, and develop increasing autonomy in their professional and personal lives. In his work in facilitating change in organizations, Lawyer believes that creating dignity, meaning, and community in the workplace enables people to support and be committed to the idea behind their work. In this way work becomes satisfying, and both the organization as a whole and its members learn and develop.

In 1976 Lawyer founded Henneberry Hill Consultants, Inc., and currently serves as its president. It is an association of professional consultants dedicated to helping individuals, groups, and organizations improve their overall effectiveness in achieving their interests and goals. As a process consultant, he serves clients in education, business, government, social service, and church-related systems.

Prior to his entry into the consulting business, Lawyer managed an international business in which he pioneered the principle that leadership's primary task is to build trust, promote learning from experience, and enable people and work teams to achieve autonomy. These concepts were introduced in three of seven foreign manufacturing plants and one major domestic manufacturing plant.

Lawyer has a special interest in the development of models and skills for conflict management and interest-based negotiation. He has, in collaboration with others, published five books in the field of conflict resolution and change. He has been teaching three courses in Syracuse University's Annual Summer Institute on Creative Conflict Resolution since 1979.

Introduction

The frameworks presented in this book have proven useful in enabling parties to communicate effectively with one another, to anticipate and head off potential conflict, and to manage conflict once it emerges. They apply in both interpersonal and group settings and will greatly enhance the school administrator's ability to ensure that the human interaction around differences is constructive and productive.

Conflict is a situation or state between at least two interdependent parties, which is characterized by perceived differences that the parties evaluate as negative. This often results in negative emotional states and behaviors intended to control the other parties in the interaction. Although differences and conflict are inevitable among people, the negative emotional energy associated with conflict can often be prevented using these proactive strategies.

We believe that conflict, as an expression of real emotion, can serve a constructive purpose. The key is managing the conflict when it emerges using the skills of reflective listening and pacing, maintaining rapport at all times, and maintaining resourcefulness and control of your own emotions. We are suggesting that the emotion associated with conflict not be blocked in any way. Further, we are saying that, with the use of skill and the strategies and models presented in this book, human interaction can be encouraged and maintained in a constructive mode.

Agreement Management

The lack of clear agreements or the lack of follow-through on agreements made is the cause of a significant amount of conflict in schools. An agreement is a commitment to act in a designated way in the future to meet another's needs. With sound agreements in place, the parties involved know what to expect of one another and are more likely to live out these expectations.

In this chapter we present a model for agreement management and an effective process for using assertion to confront lapsed agreements. Our emphasis is on a constructive model for preventing conflict in the first place. It is proactive.

Agreement management enables you to get your needs met when your needs depend on others. We believe much of the conflict that emerges in society is eliminated when people have the ability to set and manage agreements well.

The Agreement Management Model

You cannot make another person do what you want. You can only create the context and environment in which the other will choose to act in ways that serve your interests. A framework for

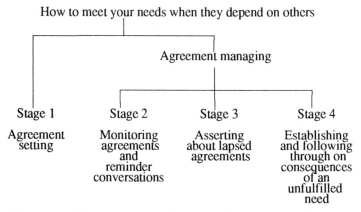

Figure 1.1. The Agreement-Setting and Management Model

enabling people to cooperate in meeting one another's needs is presented here as a model for agreement setting and management. The model is shown in Figure 1.1.

The elements of the model are described in the following sections along with suggestions on how to use the model.

Agreement Setting

The purpose of agreement setting is to get an agreement, either with another person or a group. The four steps involved in setting an agreement are illustrated in Figure 1.2.

---

1. Say what you want and why.
2. Listen and clarify.
3. Identify and resolve any problems.
4. State the agreement.

Figure 1.2. The Agreement-Setting Process

Each of the steps of this stage is described in the following sections.

A one-sentence beginning:

- "I'm having difficulty . . . involves you . . . I need your help . . . "

Ensure good time to talk:

- ". . . not sure if this is a good time . . . wanted to let you know so we could find a convenient time to talk about something . . ."

Short overview of problem:

- "It's about _____."

Positive expectation:

- ". . . expect we can work it out . . . this will really help me . . . I know we can resolve it and that it will help the way we work together . . . thanks."
  Statement of "wants" and "whys":

- "A way I want to work is (x) (y) (z). I'm asking you because _____."

- "I'm not sure if I've been clear about something I want, and so I want to talk about it now to make sure there's no misunderstanding. It's about _____."

Figure 1.3. Step 1. Opening Comments

Step 1: Say What You Want and Why You Want It

This step involves stating what you want and the rationale for your wants. This means being clear about your position and the interests that underlie it. Before raising any issue with another person, you should be clear about what should be done; why the agreement should be made; who is involved; and about any specifics regarding implementation such as authority, directions, or training. The key is to know what you want. When you know what you want, you need to constructively say it to the person with whom you want an agreement. This involves opening the conversation and making a statement of your wants and why you want what you want. Some example statements for opening the conversation and making the statement of what you want are provided in Figure 1.3.

Invite reactions:

- "How do you feel about that?"
- "Do you have any problems with that?"
- "If you have any problems with doing that, I'd like to talk about it and help work things out . . . "
- "I see two problems with making it happen. I'd like to tell you what I think and then hear any problems you see . . . goal is to work it all out . . . "

Figure 1.4. Step 2. Invite Reactions

Step 2: Listen and Clarify

This step involves listening to the other(s) with whom you want the agreement. Careful reflective listening at this point in the process is essential to ensure rapport and an understanding of the other party's position and interests. To stimulate a response from the other, you can specifically invite reactions with some of the comments illustrated in Figure 1.4.

Often you can get an agreement at the completion of your listening to the other. If so, you can move to Step 4 and summarize the agreement. If resistance to working out an agreement exists, move to Step 3.

Step 3: Identify and Solve Problems

The seven-step problem-solving process elaborated in chapter 3 of Katz and Lawyer's (1993) *Resolving Conflict Successfully* is a useful tool if differences emerge. This process is summarized in Figure 1.5. In this step you are essentially using the negotiation process with the other(s) to achieve a mutually agreeable outcome.

This must be a person-person, nonadversarial problem-solving meeting. The goal is to ensure that all parties feel good about the commitment. Using problem solving at this point enables you to get your needs met and enables the other(s) to get legitimate help to resolve any problems that stand in the way. This requires an

1. Define the problem in terms of desired state (results, needs).
2. Identify all options for solution and clarify options that are ambiguous (brainstorm).
3. Evaluate alternative solutions.
4. Decide on an acceptable solution (one option or combination of options).
5. Develop an implementation/action plan (who will do what by when).
6. Develop a process for evaluating the results (include in implementation/action plan).
7. Talk about the experience (of problem solving).

Future actions:
1. Implement the solution.
2. Evaluate the result.

Figure 1.5. Seven-Step Problem-Solving Process

honest, open, respectful sharing of ideas. The problem solving can take place in the meeting or be postponed until a later time. Specific wording that can be used to invite others into problem solving is shown in Figure 1.6.

Do it now . . . if it's relevant:
- "You're saying your room clock doesn't work. Let's see how we can get around that problem . . ."

Postpone if not relevant:
- "I promise to help with that . . . later. If I agree to do that, can you . . . ?"
- "You're saying you can't get the typing to me by Thursday because you don't get it fast enough from George . . . What if I talk to George and can work that out with him? Would you have any other problems . . . ?"

Figure 1.6. Step 3. Invitation to Problem Solving

Step 4: State (Voice) the Agreement

This step involves stating the agreement clearly and eliciting a "yes" response of the other. You will need to use reflective listening to the response so that you are sure that the agreement is a sound one. You might also wish to check to make sure that there are no other problems that might get in the way.

The meeting must end with a commitment. It is this agreement that gives you the right to confront in the future if, for any reason, the agreement is broken.

Figure 1.7 offers some examples of some specific words to use in Step 4.

Uncover additional problems:

- "Anything else you can think of that might get in the way of doing (x)?"

Get agreement/commitment:

- "So, from now on you agree to . . . ?" If "YES" . . . offer thanks and appreciation.

Figure 1.7. Step 4. State the Agreement

The elaborated Stage 1 agreement-setting process is summarized in Figure 1.8.

Agreement Managing

Agreement managing is the process of holding another accountable for an agreement. This includes monitoring the agreement and asserting if the agreement is broken. This process includes the remaining three stages presented in Figure 1.1:

- Stage 2: Monitoring the agreement
- Stage 3: Asserting about lapsed and broken agreements
- Stage 4: Establishing and following through on consequences

Each of these stages is elaborated in the following three subsections.

1. Say what you want and why.
   - Opening comments
   - Statement of "wants/policies/expectations"
2. Listen and clarify.
   - Invite reactions
   - Clarify issues
3. Identify and solve problems.
   - Good faith problem solving
   - Uncover additional problems
4. Voice the agreement.
   - Get agreement/commitment
   - Summarize who is to do what by when

Figure 1.8. Stage 1. The Four-Step Agreement-Setting Process

Stage 2: Agreement Monitoring

If infringement occurs or a problem arises with the agreement, point out specifically any problem area or area of infringement. This is an opportunity to also repair any loopholes in the original agreement. Sometimes this takes the form of a reminder conversation to point out the infringement and to clarify the standard or prior agreement about behavior. This conversation can serve to clarify any misunderstandings and to provide you with the opportunity to be a resource to the other(s). If the agreement is being upheld, this is a good opportunity to reinforce the agreement by offering appreciation and/or recognition. Example statements are illustrated in Figure 1.9.

Stage 3: Assertion Meeting

If infringement occurs or a problem arises again, then hold an assertion meeting. In the assertion meeting, you might review the history of the problem and use the assertion process to work out an agreement that meets your needs. If the assertion process does not bring about agreement, use a conflict resolution strategy to obtain a resolution. Either process should result in a renewal of the

Monitoring may be necessary to help the parties involved stick to their original (Stage 1) agreement.

Recognition/Appreciation:
- When you finished (x), as we agreed, I felt appreciative . . . "

Reminder:
- "Remember that we both agreed that you would do (x) . . . "

Figure 1.9. Stage 2. Agreement Monitoring

contract or agreement on a new contract, agreement, or action plan to ensure resolution of the difficulty. The process used for the assertion meeting is set forth in Figure 1.10.

Stage 4: Decision Meeting

If infringement occurs again or the problem persists, then hold a decision meeting. In the decision meeting you might communicate to the person the need to examine the relationship itself and indicate that, if the behavior persists, the relationship will need to be modified or terminated. For example, a person working for you will need to explore the possibility of a job change, a close friend will need to change the nature of his or her relationship with you, or an associate will need to consider terminating a professional relationship.

The most challenging stage, and the stage requiring the most preparation, is Stage 3, the assertion meeting. This stage involves the careful preparation of an assertion message and the sending of the message in a respectful manner. These two areas are elaborated in the next two major headings.

Message Formulation

The emphasis in this section is on the formulation of assertion messages used to invite behavior change. The focus is on the accurate preparation of each of the parts of an assertion message. Assertion messages are used to invite another who is infringing you

1. Begin appropriately - (decent welcome) and to the point.
   - "I want to talk about . . . "
2. Refer to Stage 1 agreement.
   - . . . we both agreed . . . seemed fair to you . . .
3. Mention reminders.
   - . . . and a couple of times . . .
4. State current situation.
   - . . . now, again, yesterday . . .
5. State goal of session.
   - . . . want to stop it from happening again . . .
6. Indicate context of relationship.
   - (if good) . . . all else is fine . . . it's this one area . . .
   - (if problematic) . . . we've had many problems, this might begin to get us on the right track.
7. Send the assertion message.
   - . . . so, the problem is that:
     - When you
     - I feel
     - Because
8. Reflectively listen to the response.
9. Recycle Steps 7 and 8 until agreement is reached or prior agreement affirmed.
10. Process.

Figure 1.10. Stage 3. The Assertion Meeting Process

to alter his or her behavior. Although there are several ways of confronting problem behavior, the three-part assertion message is particularly effective in dealing with persistent problems—those behaviors that continue after several attempts have been made to change them. Well-prepared and skillfully delivered assertion messages can invite and motivate others to voluntarily change their behavior without spending time in unnecessary arguments. A three-part assertion message is the substantive part of the communication in the assertion process, illustrated in Figure 1.11. It consists of a description of (a) the problem behavior pattern, (b) your feeling about the situation, and (c) the concrete and tangible negative

Write your message here:

When you don't_____
_____as we agreed
such as_____
I feel_____
because_____.

Figure 1.11. Assertion Message Format

effect of that pattern of behavior on you and your life. The format
of the message is as follows:

1. When you do not (*problem behavior*)
2. I feel (*your feeling*)
3. Because (*the consequences to you*)

When an adequate agreement is in place, it is useful to reference
the agreement and to offer an example. The detailed format for an
assertion message is shown in Figure 1.11.

This structured format or syntax helps ensure that all three parts
of the message are included. As you gain experience with this method
of asserting to others, you will be able to develop a style that is
more natural for you and that will convey the three necessary pieces
of information in an integrated way.

Often the phrase *as we agreed* can be added to the first part of the
message to refer to the contract or agreement developed between
you and another in a prior conversation. When used, it need only
be stated the first time the assertion message is sent to the other.

The following sections present guidelines to help you develop
your ability to formulate each of the components of a three-part
assertion message.

Describing the Behavior

When another's behavior has a negative effect on your life, one
of the three things you need to communicate is a description of the
behavior that is causing you a problem. Even when a person wants
to meet your needs, it is unlikely that he or she will change a be-

havior that is bothersome to you unless he or she knows exactly what is going on that troubles you. In developing this "behavior" component of the three-part assertion message, the following guidelines are helpful:

1. Describe the pattern of behavior accurately (specify what you are seeing or hearing).
2. Reference any agreements.
3. Include a brief example.
4. Specify the right behavior, the specific behavior bothering you.
5. Avoid using inflammatory words, such as *failed to*, *neglected*, and so on.
6. Avoid using generalizations, universal quantifiers such as always, never, all, constantly, and so on.
7. Avoid using adjectives to elaborate the behavior.
8. Avoid using adverbs such as frequently, often, repeatedly, and regularly to elaborate the behavior.

Describing Your Feeling

The second part of the three-part assertion message is a description of the feeling effect on you. Your feeling is a single word that describes your internal state as a consequence of the behavior. The feeling word needs to capture your level of emotion about the problem behavior and its effect on your life. In developing the "feeling" component of the three-part assertion message, the following guidelines are helpful:

- Use a feeling word that accurately describes your internal emotional state.
- Avoid using the same word to describe all your feelings.
- Avoid using stronger feeling words to build your case when those words do not accurately reflect your internal state.
- Avoid using "victim" words such as *hurt*, *disappointed*, or *let down*.

Describing the Negative Effect on Your Life

The third component of the three-part assertion message is a description of the negative effect the problem behavior has on you.

This is another piece of information you need to tell a person whose behavior is affecting your life in a negative way. Even when you describe the problem behavior itself accurately, if you do not communicate the problem that behavior is causing you and the negative impact the behavior has on your life, he or she is not as likely to change the problem behavior. In developing the "negative-effect" component of the three-part assertion message, the following guidelines are helpful:

- Specify the effect as concretely as possible.
- State the effect on your life.
- Avoid using reasons (only identify the essential, main consequence on you).
- Avoid exaggerating the effect or using words such as *always* or *cannot*.
- Avoid using an effect that "sounds good" but is not true.

Message Sending

After an assertion message has been thought out and carefully worded, it is important to rehearse the message and then arrange an appropriate time and place to deliver it to the person who has infringed on you.

The sequence shown below is followed when delivering the assertion message (Steps 7, 8, and 9 in the assertion process, Figure 1.10).

- Send the assertion, or "I," message ("When you ___ I feel ___ because ___").
- Silence (wait for a response or a solution).
- Use reflective listening to the other's response.
- Recycle the above three steps.
- Express appreciation for the solution or reaffirmed agreement.

Emotional Energy

When sending an assertion message, it is important for you to remember to use reflective listening to the other's response because that will help reduce defensiveness and lower his or her high energy level. Likewise, it is important for you to remember to resend

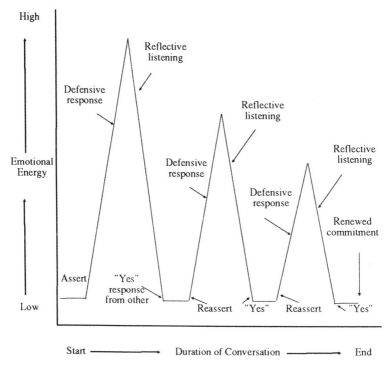

Figure 1.12. Lowering Emotional Energy Through Assertion and Reflective Listening

the assertion message after reflective listening, because the message will have a greater effect now that the other's "emotional energy" has been lowered by the reflective listening (that is, the other will hear the message more completely). Figure 1.12 illustrates the use of assertion and reflective listening skills to lower the other's emotional energy during the assertion process. You will be able to pinpoint the exact timing to reassert by getting a yes response from the other, as indicated in this figure.

Altering the Three-Part Assertion Process

The assertion message needs to be real for you and make sense to the other. Occasionally, the message might need to be altered to fit the situation. The circumstances under which you might alter the assertion message or process are the following:

- You provide additional information after which you return to the assertion process.
- The other offers you an acceptable solution after which you express appreciation.
- You receive new information from the other. In this case, you may modify your own position and solve the problem.
- The other brings up an irrelevant topic. In this case, you would listen to the content and then return to the original focus.
- The other persists in treating you inhumanely. In this case, you will alter the message or end the conversation.
- You move to stating and acting on consequences (Stage 4) when the other refuses to modify his or her behavior.

Assertion Difficulties

Some common difficulties in using three-part assertion messages are the following:

- *Undershooting or overshooting*: reporting a mild feeling of "upset" when "furious" actually fits the situation, or reporting a strong feeling when a mild one would be more appropriate.
- *Sender too much in grips of anger*: The level of anger is too high to use reflective listening effectively.
- *Forgetting to use reflective listening*: not remembering to use reflective listening to the other's defensive response.
- *Forgetting to reassert after reflective listening*: not remembering to send the message a second and third time.
- *Not asserting directly to the source*: sending the message to a friend when another is the infringing party.

Physical Components of Assertion

In assertion it is essential that your physiology be congruent with your verbal messages. With both your words and physiology, you want to communicate that the issue is important to you and that you want both yourself and the other party to attempt to deal with the issue now.

Listed below are a number of factors that contribute to the overall effectiveness of an assertion. In sending an assertion message, consider the following factors carefully to be sure they support your intended message:

- *Eye contact*: Use direct, concentrated eye contact that communicates: "This is important to me."
- *Posture*: Lean slightly toward the other, with a posture that communicates the seriousness of the message.
- *Gestures*: These should support the force of the communication.
- *Facial expression*: This needs to be congruent with the message.
- *Voice*: Use the appropriate tone, rate, volume, and inflection.
- *Timing and location*: Select the right time and location to ensure privacy and freedom from interruption.
- *Content of message*: Use the three-part "I message" rather than "you message." Use reflective listening to all responses.

Handling Difficult Assertion Defenses

In some situations, the other responds to an assertion message in a nonverbal way, offering no words to use reflective listening to. In each of these cases, you need to use reflective listening, not to the words but to what you observe in the other's behavior, for example, silence, leaving, disgust, crying, or laughter. Some examples are illustrated in Figure 1.13.

Listening to these more difficult responses will often result in reengagement and the offering of some words by the other person. You can then continue to use reflective listening and proceed to a successful resolution of the assertion.

Conclusion

School administrators make many agreements during every school day. The agreement management model, which consists of specific strategies for agreement setting and agreement managing, is a powerful conceptual framework to help facilitate agreements that are more explicitly understood and monitored by each of the affected parties. When problems arise from noncompliance to the terms of the agreement, the model provides a strategy to attempt to work

1. *When the other is silent.*
   - "I can see you're really overcome by what I've said."
   - "You're so jarred right now you can't think of anything to say."
   - "I've sort of wiped you out right now."
2. *When the other leaves.*
   - "You're so upset by this that you're walking out."
   - "You really want to get away from me right now."
   - "You're so concerned about what I've said that you're leaving."
3. *When the other looks disgusted.*
   - "It seems to you as if I'm making a big thing out of nothing."
   - "I really seem thin-skinned to you."
   - "It's as if I'm making a mountain out of a molehill."
   - "You think I've got a lot of nerve bringing this up when I've got my faults, too."
4. *When the other cries.*
   - "This is really upsetting for you."
   - "You're feeling extremely hurt by this."
   - "I've really embarrassed you."
   - "My message brought a lot of pain for you."
5. *When the other laughs.*
   - "This all seems pretty silly to you."
   - "I appear pretty funny to you."
   - "You seem to find my concerns quite amusing."

Figure 1.13. Examples of Reflective Listening Responses to Special Situations

out the problem directly and clearly. Well-articulated and well-managed agreements will significantly reduce the amount of conflict in schools and in society.

Facilitation

Administrators spend a significant amount of time in working with groups to achieve particular outcomes. The ability to work with groups effectively contributes to the efficient and successful functioning of the school. The process of assisting a group to achieve its outcomes is called facilitation. High-quality facilitation produces high-quality results and prevents conflict from escalating around differences.

Differences naturally emerge in group work. In well-facilitated groups, these differences are handled by using planning, a clear structure, and an attention to the process of the group as it unfolds.

This chapter focuses on the function and the process of facilitation and then addresses how you can perform that function and engage in the process as an administrator, in the role of a designated facilitator, a chairperson, or a group member.

Facilitation as a Function

Facilitation is a function performed by an individual that assists a group in meeting the group's outcomes. As a function, facilitation is acting on behalf of the group to enable the group to accomplish the results decided and agreed on by the group members. Effective facilitation usually results in increased group members' satisfaction because their outcomes are met with greater ease. Any group member can perform the facilitative function to move a group in the direction of its outcomes. Individuals who provide the facilitative function for a group do four primary things, which are listed below.

1. *Provide structure for the group's interaction.* The structure involves planning the meeting and making physical arrangements to ensure that the group meets its outcomes. Such details as furniture, seating arrangement, schedule, audiovisual equipment, writing material, and breakout rooms are examples of structure. The individual who is facilitating helps specify the agenda, the outcomes, the order in which the agenda will be addressed, and how the work will be handled and by whom.

2. *Influence the process of the group.* The process is how the group does its work in accomplishing its outcomes. The individual facilitating the process of the group constructively influences how group members interact. Process includes such matters as who talks to whom, how controversial issues are addressed, and how decisions are made. The individual facilitating can help a group attend to its process by assisting the group in deciding on norms and reaching agreements about how the group will do its work. Facilitation also includes inviting the group to examine its process at various times. An individual facilitating might also offer observations about how the group is doing its work.

3. *Focus the group on its task.* The task of the group is the achievement of its outcomes. The individual facilitating the task of the group provides tools for accomplishing work. These include force field analysis, problem solving, root cause analysis, as well as other technical analysis tools for examining the current situation. In task work, a person performing these duties might influence the content work of the group by such actions as bringing in new information, summarizing similarities and differences, suggesting an option

that meets at least some of everyone's interests, or by attempting to get closure on a particular effort.

4. *Enable the group to manage its emotion (feelings).* The emotion of a group is the feeling state of the members and group as a whole. The person providing this function reflectively listens to the group members as individuals and names the feeling state of the group as a whole. When the emotional state of a group is publicly named, the group as a whole can work constructively with the emotion and reconnect with the group's task.

The primary motivation of persons facilitating the work of a group is to act on behalf of the group and make it easier and more satisfying for the group to do its work and achieve its outcomes. By paying attention to both the content of the interaction and the way the content is being communicated, people acting in a facilitative way have more influence in a group than those members who focus exclusively on the issues.

The prime overall function of a person who chooses to facilitate is to enable the members of the group to discover their common ground and to achieve their outcomes by engaging in an open, participative, and democratic process. Whatever the outcomes, when a group can reach consensus on a decision, the result is more satisfying and the group members are more committed to it.

Facilitation as a Process

Facilitation is also a process. As a process, facilitation aids a group in meeting its outcomes. The process may involve conducting a meeting, solving a problem, or making a decision. The person selected to perform this special leadership role is called a "facilitator." Groups experiencing conflict and tension often find it beneficial to have a facilitator assist in directing the communication flow during the meeting, establish procedures that involve group members, and help group members identify more closely with the decision(s) made. The facilitator role may be filled by a trained communicator who is outside the group or by any group member.

Facilitators are not chairpeople to whom comments are addressed nor parliamentarians who interpret and enforce rules. Instead, they are unobtrusive enablers who use skills to assist group members in deciding what they want to accomplish in a meeting and then help the group to achieve those outcomes. The facilitator accomplishes this delicate task by focusing primarily on the process of human interaction. This involves careful design as well as initiating process suggestions, which the group may accept or reject during the meeting. At no time does the facilitator make decisions for the group or take on functions that are the responsibility of the group. A good facilitator helps participants be aware that they are in charge, that it is their business that is being conducted, and that each person has contributions to make to the group. Facilitators make it easy for a group to do its work and to achieve its outcomes.

Principles of Facilitation

Facilitation works the best when the following principles are modeled by the facilitator:

1. *Participation*
   - There is equal participation.
   - Planning is open and shared.
   - The agenda is designed to meet the group's outcomes.
   - Hierarchical structures are not imposed during the meeting.
2. *Responsibility*
   - Each person is responsible for his or her own behavior.
   - The facilitator is responsible for the process.
3. *Cooperation*
   - All work together to achieve the outcomes.
4. *Honesty*
   - All group members are encouraged to state their thoughts and feelings openly, honestly, and constructively.
   - The facilitator models and sets a tone of honesty.

In small groups that meet regularly, the function of facilitation may be shared on a rotating basis, but in large meetings, or in meetings that are anticipated to be difficult, a clearly designated facilitator is needed. Co-facilitators, when appropriate, are able to take turns facilitating and giving support to each other. The person not actively facilitating can pay more attention to the emotional atmosphere of the meeting and nonverbal cues, while his or her co-facilitator is performing the facilitating function.

The choice of a person to facilitate is important and should not be handled by default or by personal favors. When choosing a person to facilitate, it is important to keep certain specific criteria in mind. An effective facilitator will

1. Have little (or less) emotional investment in the meeting and/or issue than do other group members
2. Be able to encourage others to participate
3. Have the ability to test agreement
4. Be trustworthy, trusting, respectful, and caring
5. Have a general overview of the task or goal for the meeting
6. Have sufficient energy and attention for the job at hand and the courage to push the meeting along to stay within time limits

Facilitating conversations that involve differences are typically more difficult. In these instances, it is useful to keep six key principles in mind. These six principles are especially useful for facilitators in dealing with differences in group settings.

Principle 1: "People are doing the best they can with resources they have at the present moment."

Even though group members may be hostile or dysfunctional, they are offering their best at that moment and are protecting themselves. This awareness should lead the facilitator to respect everyone in the group.

Principle 2: "Develop and maintain rapport with every group member at all times."

If there is a break in rapport, it is the facilitator's obligation to regain rapport with the group member and the group as a whole.

Principle 3: "Whenever the group gets bogged down or sidetracked from its agenda, focus the discussion on what is happening at the present moment."

This can be done by the facilitator's intervention, indicating her or his concern or frustration with the situation, and by asking if anyone else in the group shares the same thoughts or feelings.

Principle 4: "When a conflict arises, the first step is to reflectively listen to the negative emotion. After the conflict is managed, determine if it involves needs or beliefs."

A need centers around something that affects an individual in a tangible way—it usually involves time, property, money or health. A belief is something that is important to you and is intangible.

Principle 5: "When differences involve needs, they usually revolve around positions and not interests."

A position is what a person wants. An interest is what caused the person to decide what she or he wants.

It should be noted that, in disputes, the facilitator should focus on interests, not positions. The most powerful move is to separate positions and interests. Use statements such as "Help me to understand what having that does for you."

Principle 6: "Always listen, never defend."

In the area of beliefs especially, the facilitator needs to listen so that he or she can summarize the group members' beliefs to their satisfaction.

Some Practical Steps for Facilitation

Effective facilitation can be enhanced by the use of specific steps or strategies to assist group work. The following facilitative strategies will help the group members work constructively and productively.

1. Invite each member to participate during the session.
   - Extend an invitation to each group member to contribute at the start of the meeting and during evaluation and closure.
   - If deemed appropriate, use a facilitative process such as a "whip" or "go around" to make sure that each person has an opportunity to participate in the discussion.
   - Ask open-ended questions.
2. Invite elaboration.
   - Request a person to "say more" on a particular topic.
   - Seek examples illustrating a given subject or point from group members.
3. Employ reflective listening appropriately.
   - If a communication seems unclear, check it out by restating in your own words the essence of the communication.
   - If appropriate, reflect the feelings a member has expressed.
4. Use specifying questions to improve the quality of the information offered by participants.
   - "What specifically . . ."
   - "How specifically . . ."
5. Plan and monitor time.
6. Summarize the sharing or discussion.
   - Pull together related ideas.
   - Restate suggestions made.
7. Design the meeting carefully in advance.
8. At the meeting, present and gain agreement on outcomes and evidence.
9. Use the relevancy challenge when the discussion gets off track, that is:
   - "Can you help me understand how what you're saying now relates to what we agreed to talk about?"

Handling Special Situations in the Group

Three behavior patterns tend to hinder the effectiveness of a group: A group allows one of its members to dominate, a group allows one or more of its members to remain silent, a group allows one or more of its members to engage in negative commenting. The following helpful hints will give facilitators effective strategies for dealing with difficult situations.

The Dominating Participant

Step 1. When the facilitator observes a single person dominating the discussion, intercept the conversation by listening to the dominating individual's observations, that is, check out your understanding of the participant's perspective on the matter. Then offer to the group the following invitation: "Does anyone else have a view on this issue/topic?" If there is no response, the facilitator can then redirect the subject under consideration.

If Step 1 fails, then the facilitator moves to the next procedure.

Step 2. The facilitator asserts calmly and firmly by addressing the dominating person in words like these: "You have said quite a lot on this topic. I would like to hear what some others have to say about the matter." Then the facilitator invites several others to offer their contribution.

If Step 2 fails, the facilitator moves to the next strategy.

Step 3. The facilitator focuses the group on what is happening in the present moment. The facilitator observes what is happening in the group, summarizes it, and then tests the group with a question: "Do you wish to continue in this fashion?"

For example, the facilitator might say, "I have observed in the last 10 minutes that only two people have spoken. Several others have remained silent. Do you wish to continue in this way?"

The facilitator stays out of the subsequent discussion and avoids directing it.

The Silent Participant

The facilitator might use any one of the following procedures during a meeting to engage the silent, reticent group member:

1. Intercede in the conversation and invite the silent person to participate with this or a similar invitation: "N, I'm interested in your perspective on this topic."
2. Address the group with "Would those who have not yet spoken care to speak on the topic?"
3. Observe the silent participant's physiology and remark, "N, you seem concerned. Would you care to share your thoughts or feelings with the group?"
4. On a specific topic, indicate to the group that on this particular issue the procedure will be to move around the room and to invite each person to contribute without anyone else making comments. Any person can pass. Doing this about once every meeting will at least require that the silent person indicate a desire to pass. It also provides a less threatening atmosphere for the reticent person who may fear her or his comments will be criticized or ridiculed by the others.

The Negative Participant

The facilitator should listen to the participant who makes strong negative comments about a person or issue and then use the relevancy challenge (see p. 23 #9) to invite the person to return to the discussion of material related to the group's outcome. If this negative person persists, then offer to meet privately with him or her after the meeting and return to the agenda.

Effective facilitation is both a critical function and process for productive and efficient group work. Educational administrators need to make sure that the function is being fulfilled whenever groups get together to achieve particular outcomes. The administrator should be prepared to occupy this important role if the need arises.

Meeting Management

The positive impact of facilitators is enhanced significantly by effective meeting management. Much of the work of groups in schools takes place in formal meetings, often initiated by an educational administrator. Planning, preparation, and designing and providing a framework for meetings are all critical elements in ensuring successful meetings that efficiently use limited resources. Meetings that are well organized, efficient, and productive will be well appreciated by school personnel now doing double duty focusing on school reform as well as on their regular assignments.

Teachers are especially frustrated and angry with time lost in meetings that accomplish little. The feelings lead to dissatisfaction with the system and to conflict. Well-run meetings that accomplish prescribed outcomes prevent these feelings from occurring.

Meeting Planning

When planning a meeting, it is important to recognize and be clear about your principal reason for holding a meeting. Among the legitimate reasons for holding a meeting are the following:

- Present or exchange information
- Analyze a specific situation
- Identify specific needs, interests, and concerns of the group
- Problem solving
- Decision making
- Address the social needs of group members

The outcome for some meetings can include several of the functions listed above. The group may want information on a problem, a chance to analyze it, an opportunity to raise concerns, the possibility of generating and exploring alternative options, and the authority to make a decision on the question at hand.

The principal reasons for holding meetings are elaborated below.

Exchange information. An information exchange meeting focuses on sharing knowledge, news, or advice among the people involved. Its outcome is to ensure understanding of what is going on. This type of meeting may take several forms:

1. Some meetings are briefings, where one person or a team of persons provides a group new information.
2. Another form of information exchange takes place when individuals representing the larger group or public convey their information to a smaller entity, perhaps a decision-making body. Public hearings where citizens are asked to present their viewpoints on a particular issue are an example.
3. A third model of information exchange occurs among peers. Here, no one person may have all the information, and it is necessary to compile all the knowledge held by the group members to get a total picture of the issue at hand. The goal at this type of meeting is to pool information and to educate the entire group.

Information-sharing meetings may be held as independent sessions with the sole purpose of exchanging knowledge or news, or they may be part of a larger meeting process in which analysis and decision making may occur.

Analyze a specific situation. An analysis meeting is intended to bring about a detached understanding of a given problem or situation. Its outcome is understanding of a particular issue or situation. Examples are meetings to clarify why a particular work team is not performing satisfactorily or why a school has selected a particular site for certain activities. It is important to note that the desired outcome of an analysis meeting is not a decision but an understanding of the situation.

Identify specific needs, interests, and concerns. These meetings are held to make public the needs and interests that a meeting's participants think should be taken into account in solving problems, as well as the obstacles that must be overcome to reach a satisfactory solution.

When the purpose of a meeting is to move from information exchange to a final decision, the various needs of the group participants must be identified and considered. An example of a meeting to gather needs and concerns is a public hearing to determine the desirability and feasibility of a particular project. Citizens argue for or against a specific proposal because it meets or does not meet their needs. Their concerns are directly related to their needs, and any proposed solution to a problem must meet a minimum number of needs to receive group support.

Problem solving. A problem-solving meeting is intended to identify the problem and to develop options for a solution. This may be done in separate meetings or as part of a larger problem-solving process. The outcome is an action plan. It is enriched by examining the maximum number of alternative solutions.

Decision making. A decision-making meeting is intended to reach a high-quality solution to a particular dilemma. In this meeting, the group determines and selects the best option available from those identified, using an appropriate decision-making process.

Address the social needs of group members. Not all meetings are task or product oriented. The informal breakfast meeting or the weekly social hour after school where group members talk about their personal lives may be as important to the completion of a task as any of the previously described forms of meetings. Interaction to meet social needs is invaluable in setting the tone for task-oriented group interaction, promoting trust, improving communication, and building a sense of "belonging" in the group.

Remember, it is important to be clear about the purpose of the particular meeting and to publicize that purpose in advance to people invited to participate. In this way, the attendees will be better prepared to be actively involved in achieving the goals of the meeting and will be able to evaluate its success.

Meeting Preparation

Meeting preparation should take place far enough in advance of the actual meeting to allow enough time for adequate planning. One of the most important facilitation tasks is preparation. Meeting preparation falls into the following five categories of activities:

1. Define the outcome(s) (goal or purpose).
2. Determine who should be there.
3. Make logistical arrangements.
4. Plan the meeting.
5. Notify participants.

The five steps in preparing for meetings are elaborated below.

Defining the outcome(s) (goal or purpose). The six overall reasons to hold a meeting are to exchange information, to analyze a specific situation, to identify the needs and concerns of group members, to analyze and to solve a problem including the generation of alternatives, to make a decision or to build a consensus, and to meet the social needs of the group's members. Some meetings will focus on only one of these purposes, whereas others will encompass more than one element.

The individual(s) planning a meeting should identify outcomes for the entire meeting and a particular outcome for each major agenda item. For example, imagine that you are planning for a weekly staff meeting. The general purpose of the meeting is to bring each of the staff members up to date on the others' activities and to determine staff roles for an upcoming new project. The meeting planner will initially structure the overall outcome as "understanding of mutual support required." Each agenda item will have a different outcome. The outcomes for the two agenda items might be "information on current activities understood" and "decision on staff roles made." The agenda will have to be structured so that the group can achieve both outcomes.

Determining who should be there. After reviewing the goals and purposes of a meeting, the meeting planner, in consultation with the group or its leader, should decide who should be present. Some considerations include the following: Who needs to be at the meeting to present necessary information? Who needs to hear the information? Who must be present to make a decision? Is presence at the decision-making meeting a prerequisite for implementing the decision?

Making logistical arrangements. Logistical arrangements are important for setting the tone of the meeting. Areas to consider include type of facility needed, seating arrangements, time and location of meeting, and pre-meeting publicity.

Some considerations regarding time and location include the following:

- Providing adequate time to complete the agenda
- Selecting a time of day when people are fresh and attentive
- Setting time limits on the meeting so that the decision making is not left in the hands of those who have the stamina to outlast their fellow group members
- Establishing a time that is convenient for the people involved
- Choosing a central and convenient location

Planning the meeting. When the outcomes for the meeting have been set and the participants identified, the meeting planner must plan the meeting in consultation with the decision makers or group members. General considerations in agenda planning include the following:

- Covering all the topics that should be discussed
- Allowing adequate time for questions and discussion of agenda items
- Having available all supplementary facts and materials necessary for making decisions
- Developing a constructive tone in the meeting
- Designing a process that will achieve the outcome and will enable participants to feel successful

Notifying participants. Participants need to be notified well in advance of the meeting so that they will have adequate time for preparation. Any prework as well as the agenda and the outcomes may be provided to participants to aid in their preparation

Meeting Design

The guiding principles of designing a meeting are careful advance preparation, adaptation of an array of facilitative techniques to meet the unique needs of the group, and active involvement of the group members in the meeting.

The key to designing a meeting that will have the greatest likelihood of meeting the group's need lies in the meeting planner's ability "to collect information and think diagnostically" prior to the meeting. You will find that effective advance preparation and analysis of the information the group has volunteered can give considerable insight into problems, needs, and opportunities and will greatly aid in designing an effective and appropriate meeting.

Designing a meeting can be facilitated by breaking the process down into two phases: preparatory design (the broad outline or overview of the intervention) and detailed design (plans covering the specific activities or blocks of time within the total intervention).

A Meeting Framework

Your detailed design will give you a "step-by-step" process for helping you and the group achieve the group's outcomes for the meeting. It is also useful to have an overall framework by which you can organize the process and maintain focus on the outcomes. A particular framework that we have found effective and helpful is known by the acronym PEGASUS (Laborde, 1987, pp. 116-122). It involves the seven steps described below.

Step 1 (P): Present outcomes. The best way to present the outcome(s) is to write them on newsprint so that all participants have a visual as well as an auditory representation of them.

Step 2 (E): Explain evidence. The evidence sets forth the criteria by which all participants will know that the outcome(s) were met. These criteria are best expressed in hear, see, feel data.

Step 3 (G): Gain agreement on outcomes. Gain agreement on the outcomes for the meeting. This means checking with each person individually to make sure he or she agrees. Agreement can be verified by the facilitator through a glance and confirmed through a verbal response.

Step 4 (A): Activate sensory acuity. Sensory acuity in meetings involves spotting incongruency. (*Congruency* means that all parts of an individual's personality are in agreement.) When the facilitator uncovers incongruence, he or she needs to (a) decide to resolve it, (b) ascertain that it is not relevant to the outcome, or (c) attend to it later. Most incongruities are a tip-off for a hidden agenda. Generally, it is most useful to focus on what is going on in the moment and confront the hidden agenda with respect, for example, "You seem to have some difficulty with that point. Could you elaborate?"

Step 5 (S): Summarize each major decision. Summarizing each decision as it is made allows everyone to keep track of where the group is in the meeting and what progress has been made toward the outcome.

Step 6 (U): Use reflective listening and the relevancy challenge. Reflective listening is taking in information, forming an hypothesis, and checking it out with the speaker. In facilitating the work of groups, you need to listen to individuals, themes, differences, similarities, and the group as a whole. The relevancy challenge is "How is this relevant?" The purpose of its use is to keep all discussion on the topic and focused toward the outcome. The challenge can be appropriately softened, for example, "Can you help me understand how what you are saying relates to our outcome?"; "I'm wondering how what you said helps us move toward our outcome"; or "I'm curious about. . . ."

Step 7 (S): Summarize the next step(s) (at the end of the meeting). This summary answers the question "Were the agreed on outcomes met?" This involves the following three steps: (a) Summarize the major decisions, (b) summarize the meeting result in terms of the outcomes achieved, and (c) identify and gain agreement on the specific next steps to be taken.

The educational administrator can significantly enhance the success of group meetings by adequately planning, preparing, designing, and providing a framework for the overall process. Although these tasks take considerable time and effort, school systems will be well rewarded by having meetings that are efficient in use of time and resources, and are effective not only in meeting particular outcomes but also in developing a strong "team" approach to the overall functioning of the school.

Immediacy

Immediacy is an invitation to examine what is happening in the present moment from your perspective. Immediacy enables you, as an educational administrator, to keep a conversation from dwelling on past negative feelings or worrying about what might be happening in the future. Immediacy enables you to focus on the present.

We believe that when you can focus a conversation on the present you increase the likelihood of speaking and listening to negative feelings with precision. When negative feelings are heard in the present moment, healing takes place. When conversations are conducted with immediacy, the escalation of conflict is minimized. The ability to communicate in the "here and now" is critical to the success of an educational administrator. Communicating in the here and now tends to prevent conflict from emerging because the emotions can be dealt with and attended to as they emerge. The word *immediacy* was first named by Gerard Egan (1976, p. 200). He refers to immediacy as "here-and-now" communication. It is a term used to describe a multifaceted skill of direct communication.

Communicating in the here and now with another means your ability to be fully present, to take in all the physiological cues, to use reflective listening well, and to share your thoughts and feelings as you experience them. This ability to be fully open and honest is the basis for trust. Being trustworthy and trusting is essential for learning from experience and for building autonomy in individuals and in groups.

Immediacy is important in both one-on-one and group contexts. In a group setting, immediacy requires that you are sensitive to what is happening in a group that goes beyond the task at hand. As a group is focusing on a particular task, it is useful to pay attention to what is happening from moment to moment in the group's life. Personal and interpersonal dynamics and the growth and development of the group as a whole will go on in every group and, if not attended to, will interfere with the accomplishment of the task.

Egan delineates two kinds of immediacy, "relationship immediacy" and "here-and-now immediacy." Relationship immediacy is the ability to discuss directly with another person your perceptions of your overall relationship with the other. Here-and-now immediacy refers to the ability to communicate with another your perceptions of what is happening to you in the relationship in the present moment. Figure 3.1 illustrates some examples of immediacy.

Relationship immediacy:

- "Joyce, I'm valuing our professional relationship. I especially am enjoying the way we are co-facilitating the shared decision-making meeting."

Here-and-now immediacy:

- "John, I'm hearing a cynical edge in your voice and I'm thinking it's aimed at me. I'm not sure cynical is the right word but the tone seems negative. I feel uneasy and would like to know what's going on."

Figure 3.1. Examples of Immediacy

Egan makes a distinction between relationship immediacy and here-and-now immediacy to emphasize the concern that some people make unwarranted generalizations about the quality of a relationship from a single interpersonal transaction rather than keeping the overall quality of the relationship in perspective. According to Egan, immediacy has three requirements: (a) perception, (b) skill, and (c) courage.

Perception

Perception involves sensory acuity: taking in both the verbal and nonverbal cues of another in conversation and internalizing them so that you know what is happening from moment to moment.

Skill

The skills used in immediacy include self-disclosure, feedback, and assertion. Using these particular communication skills requires reflective listening. Reflective-listening skills enable you to put your perceptions or understandings of another's thoughts and feelings into words and to reflect back to the other what he or she has said to check out, or to be sure of, your perceptions.

The first essential skill of immediacy is self-disclosure. Self-disclosure involves being willing and being able to be open and honest about your thoughts and feelings and also to be sensitive to how much self-disclosure is appropriate in a given situation to promote rather than retard the relationship.

The second important skill of immediacy is feedback. Feedback involves providing another with information about their behavior. Feedback is sensory-specific information that accurately describes what you see and hear another person doing.

The third skill of immediacy is assertion. Assertion is expressing yourself to stand up for your human rights without infringing on the rights of others. It involves expressing your thoughts and feelings to another to achieve your outcome without infringing on another, damaging your relationship with the other, or injuring his or her self-esteem. Assertion has a confrontation or challenging quality about it and hence is an act of intimacy that demands intimacy from the other.

When another is confronted by an immediacy statement, he or she may respond defensively or deny that your perception is correct. Then, of course, reflective listening is very important; you can hear the other's defensive response and bring his or her energy level down so that the other is again able to hear your perception or assertion.

Success with immediacy depends on sophisticated communication skills. We cannot afford to be ineffective with immediacy if we want to develop quality relationships.

Courage

Immediacy demands the skill, the willingness, and the courage to be assertive: to state your thoughts and feelings in the here and now in such a way as to be respectful of the other person while inviting him or her to a behavior change. By confronting minor annoyances and vague uneasy feelings as they arise, the atmosphere surrounding a relationship is kept direct and open. In this way, minor annoyances do not fester and build into major irrational "blowups."

A Framework for Feedback and Self-Disclosure

Offering feedback and self-disclosure in a context of immediacy prevents the escalation of conflict. Understanding the distinction between feedback and self-disclosure is critical to its effective use. The distinctions are the following:

Self-disclosure: statements that reveal my thoughts and feelings at the moment. Self-disclosure is about me.
Feedback: statements that reveal my perceptions of what I see and hear. Feedback is sensory-specific information about you.

Neither feedback nor self-disclosure carry or imply any judgment about the other.

The process of giving and receiving feedback can be illustrated through a model called the Johari Window (Luft, 1984; see Figure 3.2). The model was originally developed by two psychologists, Joseph Luft and Harry Ingham, for their program in group process. The model can be looked on as a communication window through

	Known to self	Not known to self
Known to others	1 Open	2 Blind
Not known to others	3 Hidden	4 Unknown

Figure 3.2. The Johari Window

Source: From *Group Processes: An Introduction to Group Dynamics* (p. 60) by Joseph Luft, by permission of Mayfield Publishing Company. Copyright © 1984 by Joseph Luft.

which an individual gives and receives information. It is a useful framework to conceptualize the distinction between feedback and self-disclosure.

Quadrant 1, the area of free activity, or open area, refers to behavior and motivation known both to self and to others.

Quadrant 2, the blind area, is where others can see things in ourselves of which we are unaware.

Quadrant 3, the avoided or hidden area, represents things we know but do not reveal to others (such as a hidden agenda or matters about which we have sensitive feelings).

Quadrant 4, the area of unknown activity, is the region where neither the individual nor others are aware of certain behaviors or motives. This area is often referred to as an individual's unconscious.

By using the model, you can come to know more about yourself by receiving "feedback" from others. This reduces the blind area and increases the area of free activity (see A in Figure 3.3). You can also increase the public area by expressing your thoughts and feelings to another or the group (self-disclosure). This reduces the hidden area and increases the area of free activity (see B in Figure 3.3). The unknown area also may be reduced by unexpected insights from the unconscious.

The enlargement of the public area, or area of free activity, means that data about an individual's attitudes and behaviors are made available both to him or her and to the group. Thus the potential

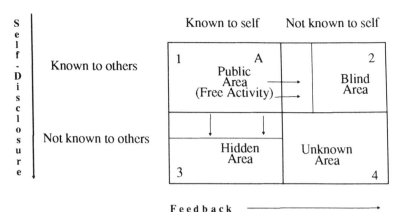

Figure 3.3. Feedback and Self-Disclosure

Source: From *Group Processes: An Introduction to Group Dynamics* (p. 60) by Joseph Luft, by permission of Mayfield Publishing Company. Copyright © 1984 by Joseph Luft.

for constructive interaction between individuals and the group as a whole is raised to a new level.

Directly related to the enlargement of the public area is the issue of how group members deal with what is called "unfinished business." Unfinished business may be illustrated briefly by considering the case in which a group participant becomes aware of a feeling or thought about self or others and does not disclose this information. This enlarges the hidden area and accumulates unfinished business. That issue acts as an unresolved tension in the group, which must be resolved in order for the group to move forward with its task.

Luft (1984) suggests 12 principles that are useful in helping group members understand the significant events that occur in groups:

1. A change in any one quadrant will affect all other quadrants.

2. It takes energy to hide, to deny, or to be blind to behavior that is involved in interaction.

3. Threat tends to decrease awareness; mutual trust tends to increase awareness.

4. Forced awareness (exposure) is undesirable and usually ineffective.

5. Interpersonal learning means a change has taken place so that Quadrant 1 has grown larger and one or more of the other quadrants has grown smaller.

6. The larger the area of free activity, the more working with others is facilitated. An increased Quadrant 1 means that there are more resources and skills in the membership that can be applied to a task.

7. The smaller the first quadrant, the poorer the communication.

8. There is universal curiosity about the unknown area, but this is held in check by custom, social training, and diverse fears.

9. Sensitivity means appreciating the covert aspects of behavior—in Quadrants 2, 3, and 4—and respecting the desire of others to keep them covert.

10. Learning about group processes as they are being experienced helps to increase awareness (enlarge Quadrant 1) for the group as a whole as well as for individual members.

11. The value system of a group and its membership may be noted in the way unknowns in the life of the group are confronted.

12. A centipede may be perfectly happy without awareness, but after all, it restricts itself to crawling under rocks.

The concepts of self-disclosure and feedback are elaborated in the following sections.

Self-Disclosure

Self-disclosure is a self-presentation skill. It involves the expression of emotion in concrete terms. Appropriate self-disclosure is suitable to the setting, to the nature of the relationship, and to the outcome of the communication. Appropriate self-disclosure involves the ability to judge the depth of the disclosure that is possible or desirable in a particular situation. Appropriate self-disclosure is marked by mutuality. Mutuality is "the ability of two people to engage in direct and non-manipulative dialogue while comprehending and accepting each other's frame of reference" (Egan & Cowan, 1979). Mutuality is a desirable systems characteristic in any educational institution and an essential ingredient for community. Mutuality in human systems provides a framework within which the community's members can develop personally and professionally. Egan describes three levels of mutuality in human systems:

1. *Basic decency*: a level of mutuality that enables the members of a community to know that others accept them as they are and are willing to understand their experience from their frame of reference. This level of mutuality is basic human acceptance.

2. *Assertion*: a level of mutuality that enables the members of a community to respectively challenge one another and call one another to accountability. At this level of mutuality, people feel secure that they will feel safe in human interaction and will have access to the feedback they need for their ongoing development.

3. *Immediacy*: a level of intimacy at which community members are capable of being direct and open with one another concerning the state of the relationship and from moment to moment in their human interaction.

Feedback

Feedback is providing sensory-based information to another for the purpose of enabling another to make informed choices. In giving feedback effectively, you need to know the answers to the following three questions:

1. *Who is the feedback really about*? True feedback is information for the receiver. It is sensory specific and without judgment.

2. *Do you have an investment in the other changing*? True feedback has no requirement of change. It is only information for the receiver. Its interaction is to provide information to the receiver and to open up a "blind spot" in the receiver's behavior. It is simply a statement that says, "Here's what I see . . ." or "Here's what I hear. . . . "

When you want the other to change his or her behavior, as opposed to just saying what you see, then it is an assertion. This is the critical distinction between feedback and assertion. The following examples illustrate this distinction: "You might not know that people at the party will be dressed a lot less formally than what you're wearing. I'll see you later, I'm a little late . . . bye." (*feedback*; no agenda for the other to change). "When you wear formal dress to a casual party, I feel uncomfortable walking in with you." (*assertion*; an agenda for the other to change).

The impact of feedback is greatest when no response is required by the receiver.

3. *What is positive versus negative feedback?* True feedback is neutral, neither positive nor negative. Positive and negative are distinctions best made on the basis of *values*. If the feedback is clear, direct, and honest, then it is most likely to be perceived as positive; that is, when it has no agenda. If it is full of judgment, criticism, intent to change, and so on, then it is likely to be perceived as negative.

Once these questions are answered, and you choose to provide feedback, the following guidelines help ensure that the feedback is constructive and provides useful information to another.

Guidelines for Giving Feedback

1. *Feedback is most likely to be understood when it is given immediately after the behavior has been observed.* This is illustrated by the example "You might not be aware that you just broke into John's conversation."

The receiver of this feedback might not like what he or she heard but is much more likely to understand it than if the feedback was delayed or generalized.

2. *Feedback is more likely to be understood and accepted when it describes specific, observed behavior.* This is illustrated by the example "When Al made that remark to Pete, you seemed to come immediately to Pete's defense."

This feedback describes specific behavior. It would be even more specific if exact words were used to describe "defense." The example is better, however, than "You always seem to protect everyone." It is more likely that there would be many exceptions to the generalization. The exceptions provide ammunition for an argument and enable the receiver to avoid learning about him- or herself.

Feedback that characterizes the whole person instead of describing specific observed behavior is not very useful. "You're a very kind person." "You're a nice guy." "You're stupid." Although these statements imply the impact of the other person's behavior, they give no hint as to the action that prompted the conclusions.

Speculation about others' motives for behavior is also not useful. "You're trying to dominate the group." "You want everyone to like you." These kinds of statements indicate that the speaker believes he or she knows why others behave as they do. That is rarely true or relevant. What is important to cite in feedback is the behavior, what you see and hear.

3. *Useful feedback avoids making moral or ethical judgments about the behavior.* Words such as *right, wrong, mature, immature, good, bad, should,* and *shouldn't* express moral or ethical judgments.

Judgments about another's behavior often stimulate intellectual debates, polarize adversaries into win-lose postures, and raise defenses. Although someone can speak with complete authority about his or her own feelings, the same person is not likely to be accepted as an authority drawing conclusions about behavior.

4. *Feedback is more meaningful when it is verified by several people, not just one.* One person's perceptions and reactions may be typical for the group, or they may be unique. Therefore, it is helpful to solicit other views. This is illustrated by the example "I wonder if others saw that as I did." Thus the giver of feedback also has an opportunity to learn to what extent his or her perceptions and reactions are shared by others.

Figure 3.4 compares effective and ineffective approaches to giving feedback.

Effective feedback
- Immediate
- Specific observed behavior
- Objective

Ineffective feedback
- Delayed
- Conclusions about behavior
- Characterizations of the whole person
- Diagnosis of others' motivations
- Judgments
- One person's perceptions and reactions

Figure 3.4. Effective and Ineffective Approaches for Giving Feedback

Guidelines for Receiving Feedback

In addition to these guidelines for the giving of feedback to help ensure the feedback is constructive and useful, there are particular methods for receiving feedback that have proven useful.

1. *Feedback is more likely to be understood if the receiver listens attentively.* A typical reaction to hearing negative feedback is to stop listening and start preparing a rebuttal. Unfortunately, this prevents the receiver from hearing the whole message.

2. *Communication is completed when the receiver reflectively listens to the feedback.* If the receiver can state the essence of the message in his or her own words to the satisfaction of the sender, both know that the message got through. Using reflective-listening skills helps the receiver listen attentively and avoid "tuning out" to prepare a "rebuttal."

3. *The receiver can learn whether the feedback represents only one person's opinion or a consensus by verifying the feedback with others in the group.* In most cases there are differences, subtle or substantial, in participants' perceptions and reactions.

4. *Feedback does not require that the receiver change his or her behavior.* A participant is free to modify his or her behavior to please others but is equally free to continue behavior that displeases others. If the group standards seem to require certain behaviors or forbid others, the standards should be examined. How were they set? By whom? How are they to be enforced?

5. *The best way to get feedback is to give it.* Some group participants become concerned because they have not received feedback. They solicit it but get only vague or general responses. In most cases, the individual who is not getting much feedback has not given much. If one person is unwilling to risk giving others feedback, others will be unlikely to risk giving him or her feedback.

Figure 3.5 compares effective and ineffective approaches to receiving feedback.

Effective feedback

- Listen respectfully - using reflective listening (check it out)
- Check for consensus
- Retain autonomy
- Demonstrate willingness to give and receive feedback

Ineffective feedback

- Prepare rebuttal
- Assume understanding
- Assume uniqueness or consensus
- Submit to group pressure
- Solicit feedback while withholding own perception and reactions

---

Figure 3.5. Effective and Ineffective Approaches for Receiving Feedback

The successful communicator integrates the skill of immediacy into his or her total communication in an ongoing way. Relationship immediacy does not become a "heavy" issue because you feel free to engage in here-and-now immediacy as situations that call for it emerge. The successful communicator works at relationships without being preoccupied by them.

An administrator's ability to self-disclose and to give and receive feedback appropriately enables the building of trust and results in enhanced relationships. When communication is handled in an honest and open way, the likelihood of conflict emerging or escalating is significantly lessened.

Consensus Decision Making

One of the most effective ways to prevent conflict from emerging in schools is to create a system in which everyone in the school building, including the students, has the opportunity to influence decisions. When participative decision-making processes are in place, everyone is more likely to experience satisfaction. *Decision making* is determining a course of action from among alternatives. *Participative decision making* is decision making by members of an organization or group that enables each to experience influence in determining a particular direction. Participative decision making promotes decisions that lead to cooperation rather than alienation and conflict. Within any organization or group, decision making is recognized as the most central and important administrative function. Within groups, participative decision making builds commitment to an organization's or a group's goals.

Participative or shared decision making enables the members of an organization or group to experience influence through involvement. The level of involvement required for the members to experience influence is considerable and necessarily involves a strong commitment by the group as a whole to a participative style.

Shared decision making can most effectively take place in small groups within an organization. Complete agreement on a course of action is a desirable outcome of small group decision making in most situations. However, it is not always practical or desirable in all situations. It is necessary to evaluate the circumstances to determine what decision-making process is most appropriate.

Decision-Making Options

Listed below is the range of decision process options that are available to you as an administrator, a coach, or a leader of a shared decision-making team.

1. You make the decision yourself, using information available to you at the time.
2. You obtain the necessary information from the group members who possess it and then decide yourself. You do not assemble the group as a whole. You may or may not tell the group members what the problem is when you get the information. The role played by the group members is clearly one of providing the necessary information to you, rather than generating or evaluating alternative solutions.
3. You share the problem with the relevant group members to get ideas and suggestions without bringing them together as a group. Then you make the decision, which may or may not reflect the influence of the group members.
4. You share the problem with the group members as a whole and obtain their collective ideas and suggestions in a group meeting. Then you make the decision, which may or may not reflect the group members' influence.
5. You share the problem with the group members as a whole. Together, you generate and evaluate alternatives and attempt to reach agreement (consensus) on a decision. Your role is that of a fully participating group member or of a facilitator. You do not try to influence the group to adopt "your" solution, and you are willing to accept and implement any solution that has the support of the entire group.

A simplified form of these decision alternatives is illustrated in Figure 4.1.

1. You make decision using available information.
2. You obtain information from group members who possess it individually, then make decisions.
3. You share problem with relevant group members, obtain information, and then make decision.
4. You share problem with group as whole, obtain information, and then make decisions.
5. You use consensus. (You share problem with group as a whole, generate alternatives, use consensus process, and accept group decision.)

Figure 4.1. Decision Alternatives

Source: Adapted and reprinted from *Leadership and Decision-Making*, by Victor H. Vroom and Philip W. Yetton, by permission of the University of Pittsburgh Press. © 1973 by University of Pittsburg Press.

These group decision-making methods occur on a continuum. On the one extreme, the group leader may make the decision by him- or herself. On the other extreme, the group leader may be a full participant in a consensus decision arrived at by the group as a whole.

A critical decision-making skill is knowing how to judge the unique nature of both the decision situation and the organizational setting in which the situation occurs and determining what decision-making process (i.e., what degree of group participation in making the decision) would be best suited to the specific decision situation. Judging the nature of a decision situation is the key to making a meaningful determination about the most appropriate decision-making process. Criteria for making this judgment consist of a number of basic, interrelated questions that the school administrator must ask him- or herself about the nature and the context of any decision. These questions are set forth in Figure 4.2 (Vroom & Yetton, 1973, p. 13). The answers to these questions will give a clear indication of the most appropriate mode of decision making.

Figure 4.3 presents a conceptual model based on the above questions and is adapted from Vroom and Yetton's research on leadership and decision making. It can be used by the leader of a group in

A. Is decision critical? (If decision was accepted, would it make a difference which course of action was adopted? or, Is there a quality requirement such that one decision is likely to be more rational than another?)

B. Do you have the information you need? (Do you have sufficient information to make a high-quality decision?)

C. Do group members have sufficient additional information to result in a high-quality decision?

D. Do you know exactly what information is needed, who possesses it, and how to collect it?

E. Is necessary additional information to be found within the organization?

F. Is it feasible to collect additional information outside the organization prior to making decision?

G. Is acceptance of decision by group members critical to effective implementation?

H. If you were to make decision by yourself, is it certain that it would be accepted by the group members?

I. Are group members willing and able to base decision on the interests of the organization? (Can group members be trusted to base decision on organizational considerations?)

J. Is conflict among group members likely in preferred decision?

Figure 4.2. Decision Process Questions

Source: Adapted and reprinted from *Leadership and Decision-Making*, by Victor H. Vroom and Philip W. Yetton, by permission of the University of Pittsburgh Press. © 1973 by University of Pittsburg Press.

analyzing a particular decision situation to arrive at the best decision-making approach. The model simply facilitates the process of taking into account the cumulative impact of the administrator's responses to a number of basic questions about the decision situation with which he or she is faced. The outcome reached by responding to this series of decision questions represents the decision-making process that is most suitable in light of the leader's unique decision situation.

The Decision Process Selection Model illustrated in Figure 4.3 is not necessarily one that you should refer to in your top desk

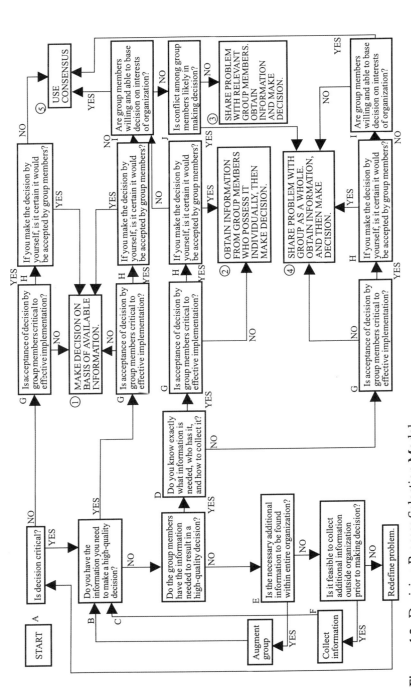

Figure 4.3. Decision Process Selection Model

Source: Adapted and reprinted from Leadership and Decision-Making, by Victor H. Vroom and Philip W. Yetton, by permission of the University of Pittsburgh Press.

© 1973 by University of Pittsburg Press.

drawer as decision situations emerge. It is a tool with which you can practice, to "fine tune" your intuitive thinking on decision making.

The decision on which decision-making procedure to use is important. The model gives you some significant criteria to use to aid you in the decision. The following five principles will also give assistance to you and your groups' efforts to select an appropriate decision-making procedure.

Guiding Principles

1. The best decisions are made when members of an organization are involved in the decision-making processes on issues that concern them.
2. The more critical the impact of a decision, the more important it is to involve those affected by the decision.
3. Consensus decisions are normally of higher quality than are decisions arrived at by other means, because they are based on the collective wisdom and creativity of the entire group.
4. The decision process selection model is an effective conceptual framework for deciding how to decide. All five decision-making alternatives are appropriate, depending on the circumstances. It is not necessarily appropriate to make all decisions by consensus.
5. The decision on how to decide is often best made by the group of which the leader is a member. This ensures that all group members are involved in the decision-making process from the inception and increases the group member's commitment to a course of action.

Consensus decisions are not appropriate for all day-to-day decision situations. Programmed decisions (i.e., those that are routine in nature and covered by policy and regulation) do not require consensus. Also, emergency situations that require an immediate response, as well as those that lie within the specific responsibility of a particular staff member, do not lend themselves to consensus decision making. Consensus decision making is most powerful and appropriate when there is no "one" correct answer. It increases communication among group members and allows the group to use all of its resources and to build investment in decisions.

Consensus Decision Making

Consensus decision making is a process whereby a group makes a decision that all the group's members can support without voting. It is an especially effective process if a high degree of commitment to a particular decision and course of action is desired.

The word *consensus* is derived from the Latin word *consentire*, "to think together." In the context of participative decision making, consensus is an agreement to implement a decision on the part of all who are "thinking together." It is a collective opinion by a group of people working together so that everyone in the group feels he or she has had a fair chance to influence the decision, understands the decision, and is prepared to support it. A tradition of consensus seeking has been a part of Quaker spirituality through its history.

In *Quaker Spirituality*, Douglas Steere (1984) provides a description of the consensus-seeking process:

> Something that might be called participative humility in the assembled members is certainly required in the Quaker decision making process for it to be able to operate effectively. In this process, whose decision I have been willing to accept, I am brought to realize that the matter has been carefully and patiently considered. I have been involved throughout the process and have had a chance at different stages in it of making my point of view known to the groups and of having it seriously considered and weighed. Even if the decision that the group feels drawn to accept may go against what I initially proposed, I know that my contribution has helped to sift the issue, perhaps to temper it, and in the course of the process, I may have come to see it somewhat differently. . . . I emerge from the meeting not as a member of a minority who feels outflanked and rejected but rather as one who has been through the process of the decision and is willing to abide by it even though my assent would not have put it in this form. (pp. 41-42)

The ultimate goal in a consensus decision-making process is to demonstrate loyalty both to the group effort and to the quality of the decision. The process works best and the decision is most easily supported when the following factors are present:

1. Those who will be significantly affected by a decision participate in making it, directly or through representatives.
2. All who have valid and relevant information are fully heard.
3. Everyone is free to express dissent and welcomes the expression of others' dissent.
4. Everyone strives hard for open-mindedness and understanding of others' views.
5. Everyone strives to avoid categorical "yes" or "no" choices, in favor of integrative decisions that accommodate the interests of all.
6. Everyone feels some obligation toward voluntary deference toward consensus in the interests of group accord without surrendering a minority view.

Consensus "Contract"

Consensus is based on the term *to consent* as in "to grant permission." Arriving at consensus is giving permission to the group to move forward with a common, shared direction. The implication of consensus is that an individual can negotiate the terms by which he or she will grant his or her permission. Each individual has the right and obligation to make his or her terms known. For the consensus "contract" to work, the individual participant must hold certain assumptions and abide by certain procedures and commitments. These include the following:

- All people are choice-making beings.
- All persons are free to disagree and to voice an opinion.
- Freedom means engaging in action by choice.
- Compromise is not always necessary.
- There is no one right answer.

To make the consensus contract work, you will need to make the following commitments:

- Explain your perception of the problem and/or issue.
- Share your feelings.
- Explain your needs and/or goals concerning the issue.
- Let others know how important this issue is to you.
- Listen to others' opinions.
- Respect others' needs and try to accommodate them.
- Negotiate differences with respect and skill.
- Participate in implementing the decision.

Roles and Responsibilities for Building Consensus

For consensus to be successful, it is important for group members, group leaders, and outside parties to all be clear about their role and responsibilities. Each must share a strong belief in the ability of members to work for the benefit of the group and to make an informed choice based on the needs of the organization or group. Those engaged in building consensus share the responsibility for consensus to work.

Responsibilities shared by group members in building consensus include the following:

1. Present your position as clearly and as logically as possible and avoid blindly arguing for your own individual judgments.
2. Reflectively listen to other members' reactions and consider them carefully before pressing your point.
3. Support only solutions with which you are at least somewhat able to agree and avoid changing your mind only to reach agreement and to avoid conflict.
4. Seek out differences of opinion and avoid "conflict-reducing" procedures such as majority vote, tossing a coin, averaging, or bargaining in reaching decisions. Differences help the group's decision-making process because they present a wide range of information and opinions, thereby creating

a better chance for the group to hit on a more satisfying solution.

5. Discuss underlying assumptions, listen carefully to one another, and encourage the participation of all members.

6. Look for the next most acceptable alternative when a discussion reaches a stalemate based on the underlying interests of all members.

The group leader can influence the success of group decision making by

1. Keeping the group focused on the outcome of the decision-making process and the group's expressed intent to reach consensus.

2. Moving the discussion to a higher level of generality if agreement is impossible at the present level. Remember that general ideas unite, specifics divide. If disagreements seem irreconcilable, moving the dialogue to a higher level of abstraction often provides a breakthrough.

3. Changing the subject and inviting the group members to consider why they are having so much trouble establishing some common ground.

4. Asking members to sort the ideas into a few categories. This may help to narrow the focus of the discussion and make agreement possible.

5. Inviting the group members to establish some criteria by which they will be able to continue. If, for example, the group is going "round and round" the problem of what kind of a sports program it wants to have, perhaps the group should step back and first decide on the criteria by which it feels a good sports program would be judged.

6. Organizing the group into small groups to reach consensus and then convening the whole group again to continue the consensus-building process.

Outside Facilitator

Consensus decision making is often assisted by a person external to the system who is asked to perform a facilitating function. Such a person can assist the group in planning and designing the meeting and help the group achieve success in reaching its outcome. Helping a group reach consensus on a controversial issue is one of the more difficult tasks that a person providing the facilitative function must perform. Chapter 2 describes the function and process of facilitation. The principles set forth in the chapter can serve as a guide in enabling a group to build consensus.

To achieve consensus, time must be allowed for all members to state their views and, in particular, their opposition to other members' views. In groups operating effectively with consensus, each member of the group is feeling understood. Group members are listening carefully to one another and are communicating effectively. In reaching consensus, differences of opinion are seen as a way of gathering additional information, clarifying issues, and encouraging the group to seek better alternatives.

Working Constructively With Disagreement

Disagreements around different points of view arise for a variety of reasons, including diverse socioeconomic experience, different political perspectives, variations in personal ethics and morality, and, occasionally, psychological problems or difficult personality traits. Disagreements and conflicts can be productive. They encourage individual and group growth and move group members to new stages of consciousness and development. However, disagreements and conflicts can also be detrimental. They can block group effectiveness by stalling the group and preventing it from acting, by dividing members against each other and by allowing opponents to defeat the group because of its indecision. It is imperative that groups operating by consensus learn to resolve disagreements and move beyond barriers to agreement.

A critical distinction must be emphasized when talking about disagreement and consensus. Consensus does not mean unanimity. It does not mean that everyone agrees with every single point of a proposal or feels equally good about the decision. It does not mean that the agreement is the best one for each individual group member. It does mean that the decision is the best for the group as a whole at a particular time in a group's development.

One or more participants can block consensus, and this should not necessarily be seen as destructive. However, blocking consensus should not be done lightly. When a group member disagrees with a proposal and wants to hold back consent, there are several guidelines that he or she should consider:

1. Block consensus only for reasons of principle, never for wording or other trivial viewpoints.
2. State objections clearly so that the group knows what the points of disagreement are and why they must find an alternative solution.
3. Explain why the issue is important. Say only what is needed for clarity. Be brief.
4. Be constructive and avoid defensiveness about disagreement. The group deserves to hear a different opinion—another viewpoint—but it also has a right to disagree.

The group has a number of options when such a strong disagreement has been voiced. These include the following:

1. The group leader or a group member can identify whether the dissenting opinion is held by an individual or a small group, whether it is an objection the whole group should consider, or whether it is one that could be worked out in a smaller part of the group. Individual and small group disagreements may sometimes be resolved through individual or small group decisions that vary slightly from the whole group's decision. These individual or small group solutions may be developed outside the whole group meeting and then presented to the whole group for its approval.
2. The leader or a group member can ask the objecting person or small group if they have any alternative proposals the whole group might consider that would overcome the objections. If no alternatives are suggested, the facilitator can ask the group to break into smaller groups to discuss the question and to develop new proposals.
3. The leader or a group member can elicit a response from each person on the question (without response or discus-

sion by other group members) and then test for consensus
again on the old proposal or a modified one.

4. The leader or a group member can ask the group to take a
   break or postpone the discussion to a later date, allowing
   people a time to consider the objection and the alternatives.

Occasionally, the objection of an individual or subgroup may be
so strong that the differing viewpoints cannot be reconciled. In this
event, there are several additional options. The leader or a group
member (a) may ask the individual or subgroup to allow the group
to record their disagreement and proceed with the majority view
or (b) may ask the individual or subgroup to "stand aside" and not
block consensus, thus allowing the group to proceed. Standing
aside can release those objecting from involvement in the implementation of the group's agreement. (The individual or subgroup
may also initiate standing aside.)

In extreme cases, the individual who disagrees may decide to
leave the group, releasing the group to move ahead. Occasionally,
when a group finds that one of its members is extremely disturbed
and repeatedly and carelessly blocks decisions, the group may decide to override the individual's objections. This situation is rare,
and the option to override should be used very sparingly. It creates
a dangerous precedent in which the group decides who is "together"
and who is not or who is "in" and who is "out."

Frequently, an agreement will not be reached the first time consensus is tested. Repeated testing and asking for proposed modifi-
cations that will meet the stated needs may be required before a
decision can be reached.

When a group is having difficulty making a decision, it may be
helpful for the group to understand why. There are many explana-
tions for a group's failure to reach agreement. Such failure can often
be attributed to one or more of the following reasons:

1. Some group members are uninformed about the content of
   the decision.
2. Some group members are doubtful about the effectiveness
   of implementation.

3. Some group members are comparing the decision with other, more attractive, options.
4. Some group members are defensive because the proposal threatens personal interests.
5. Some group members see that the decision is too costly.
6. Some group members see, because of past experience, that the decision will not work.

These reasons are usually either personal, procedural, or substantive and may occur in any phase of the decision-making process. Moving beyond these reasons for rejecting can be helped by a person understanding and performing the facilitation function in the group.

The Benefits and Limitations of Consensus

When successful, consensus is a very effective decision-making process. The process itself builds trust and a sense of team, and the decisions are frequently creative, imaginative, and of high quality. When consensus is reached, the group has achieved synergy—the group outperforms the individuals that make up the group. Consensus decision making tends to have the following positive effects:

1. Improves the quantity and quality of communication within the group
2. Allows the group to use all its resources
3. Builds commitment to decision(s)
4. Deepens a sense of mutual interdependence among participants
5. Enhances satisfaction among participants with the organization's leadership and organization as a whole
6. Establishes higher performance goals
7. Deepens motivation to accomplish results
8. Heightens satisfaction among participants with the solution and decision-making process

These benefits suggest that consensus decision making has a number of significant advantages over other decision-making processes. However, group decision making does not seem to work with all people in all situations. Some of the disadvantages are that (a) it is time-consuming, (b) it allows less control for those in authority positions, (c) indecision may be more likely and involve costs, and (d) subtle intimidation of some group members by others may occur and reduce the number of wise decisions or the commitment to the decision.

Group members and group leaders need to carefully consider the benefits and limitations of consensus and alternative decision-making procedures before deciding on a process for a particular decision. This analytical step is an important responsibility for school administrators because decision-making procedures often are key to the ownership and investment that teachers, students, and parents feel in the school. Consensus decision making, when used appropriately and effectively, is a powerful contributor to a more inclusive school system where stakeholders believe they are influential in shaping the future of the school. This belief will enhance their involvement and their sense of responsibility for the school's success. Consensus decision making is another tool in the hands of educational administrators in building a working team to help accomplish the goals and objectives of the educational system.

Mediation

The use of parties not directly involved in a conflict situation to help those with differences arrive at some settlement of their dispute is familiar to all of us. Parents, teachers, and administrators routinely act as third parties and use a variety of intervention techniques to help others settle disputes. These techniques can be grouped into three broad categories.

1. Strategies where a third party behaves as an authority figure and dictates the settlement terms of the dispute. In effect, the third party essentially acts as a judge and jury by determining and imposing a solution on the parties.
2. Strategies that essentially attempt to shelter the third party from making a decision on the dispute or becoming actively involved.
3. Strategies that allow the third party to play an active, yet facilitative role with those in a dispute. With this strategy, the third party uses a problem-solving process to assist the disputants in negotiating a mutually acceptable settlement.

The first two strategies are often used within school systems and many other organizations. The first strategy, referred to as "imposition," takes place when students, teachers, or administrators bring their interpersonal disputes to a higher authority to "impose" a solution such as ruling for one party over the other, punishing one or all parties, or dictating the terms of a compromise. The second strategy, referred to as "avoidance," is a "hands-off" approach that attempts to ignore the problem in the hope it will fade away. If this does not occur, the person in authority might instruct the parties to work it out themselves, with dire consequences awaiting them if they are unsuccessful. Although well intended and often successful at reaching an agreement, these first two strategies have some serious limitations. The first strategy encourages blame, exaggeration, and a win-lose mentality instead of an open discussion of issues and a shared responsibility for analyzing and solving the problem. In addition, in imposition, the parties are less likely to live up to the terms of the agreement because it was imposed rather than voluntarily negotiated and agreed to.

The second strategy, avoidance, encourages the parties to go "underground" with their differences. Instead of settling, they might attempt to hide the conflict and displace their angry feelings into troublesome behaviors such as absenteeism, stress-related illness, or sabotage of work quality and efficiency.

These first two strategies also convey some harmful unintended messages. They foster an attitude that conflict is "bad" and "unnatural" and needs to stop immediately by almost any means necessary. And imposition reinforces a dependency belief that only more powerful authority figures, not the parties themselves, are capable of understanding the issues and creating terms for settlement.

Mediation

Mediation is a process by which a skilled communicator assists the primary parties in directly negotiating a mutually acceptable agreement to their differences. Like imposition and avoidance, this strategy attempts to stop the unacceptable behavior. Moreover, this third approach eliminates or minimizes the possible harmful messages and consequences of the first two approaches. This method uses a third party as an outside facilitator to assist the disputants in directly negotiating a mutually acceptable settlement. The third party, known as a mediator, is responsible for the process: The parties are responsible for the content of what is discussed during the mediation meeting and retain authority and responsibility over their willingness or unwillingness to settle.

School administrators might use mediation

1. To set up an informal process to encourage disputants to talk to one another with the administrator present as a nonpartisan third party
2. For school administrators to become skilled in "managerial mediation," a formal third party process by which managers and/or supervisors assist their supervisees in the constructive handling of their disputes and differences
3. To establish a mediation program in the schools in which students, faculty, and administrators are professionally trained in mediation techniques to effectively assist others in handling disputes and differences

Although these three mediation strategies are not mutually exclusive and a school administrator could effectively promote all three options, it is important to understand some of the distinguishing characteristics of the three approaches and some of their unique benefits and limitations.

Informal Mediation

The first approach is informal, often spontaneous mediation. In this process, the administrator, acting as third party, brings the disputants together in his or her office, or in a neutral place, to talk to one another to settle their dispute in a way that is mutually acceptable. The third party in this process must remain neutral and not say or do anything that could be construed as taking sides. In fact, with this approach, the mediator talks very little except to encourage constructive behavior, asking relevant questions of all the parties and perhaps summarizing points of mutual agreement. The benefits of this approach are that the process usually takes only a few minutes, the parties are empowered to come up with their own solution, and the administrator has encouraged communication and stayed out of the punishment trap. The limitations are that gut-level issues might be avoided or "sugarcoated" because the administrator is present, the parties might be too angry and upset to talk productively to each other and solve their differences, and, without a formal process, the parties might not really believe or understand the administrator's role as mediator, as opposed to the traditional boss.

Managerial Mediation

The second approach, managerial mediation (Dana, 1989), is a more formal extension of the first model. In this approach, the administrator or supervisor makes a more deliberate decision to invite supervisees to sit down with a trained third party mediator to discuss their interpersonal conflicts and to attempt to arrive at a mutually satisfactory agreement. The mediator, who may or may not be the direct supervisor of the parties involved, sits down with each of the parties separately at a preliminary meeting. The mediator clearly articulates his or her role and expectations as well as informing the disputants of their expected role and behavior. At these private meetings, disputants have time to "vent" their feelings to the administrator and to highlight the major issues in contention from their point of view. These private meetings are followed by a face-to-face meeting in which the administrator follows a more formal and detailed mediation process. If an agreement is reached, the administrator engages in contracting, monitoring, and following up.

This more detailed, formal process has several advantages. The role of the third party, as well as the roles and expected behavior of the disputants, are clearly defined and articulated, and the parties are given "up-front" time to vent their strong feelings. Some limitations of this approach include the time investment of the supervisor and concerns around issues of confidentiality.

It is important that this method be viewed by administrators as one tool to handle interpersonal disputes between two or more task-interdependent people who are experiencing strong emotion and exhibiting behavior that is disrupting work and morale in the organization. If administrators are clear when to use, or not use, mediation, they will avoid the pitfalls of intervening in inappropriate interpersonal conflicts or using mediation as a substitute for direct and necessary supervision.

Formal Mediation

The third approach, formal mediation by trained volunteers, is becoming more popular in our schools. In this model, selected students, teachers, and administrators are formally trained in the mediation process so that they might effectively provide third party intervention support for their peers. A recognizable "Mediation Center" is often established. This model has several significant benefits as it empowers many actors to assist others in peacefully settling disputes in the schools, it gives students role models of "peacemakers," it encourages students to share responsibility for encouraging appropriate behavior in conflictful situations, and it provides opportunities to build trust and to promote respect for diversity by appropriately matching mediators to disputants. Limitations are the time and financial investment to train the mediators, and teachers and administrators yielding some of their power to impose solutions to interpersonal problems.

The Mediation Process

Although each of these three approaches requires a different degree of structure and formality dependent on the attitudes and skills of the parties and the nature of the dispute, there is a generic mediation process that is helpful to learn and adopt.

The generic process consists of six steps:

- Setting the stage
- Uninterrupted time
- Focusing the issues
- The exchange
- Generation of potential solutions
- Agreement building

This process is explicated in Figure 5.1. Even in an informal context, it is useful to make sure each of these steps is sequentially followed to some degree by the third party mediators and the disputants.

Benefits of Mediation

Mediation is a form of conflict resolution that is dramatically increasing in popularity in schools, communities, and organizations. It is an effective way to handle many interpersonal disputes and allows the people who know most about the conflict to further explore the issues and attempt to come up with a solution that they both can live with and live up to. Many of the unique advantages of mediation make it a particularly appropriate and advantageous method for administrators to encourage in a school system. Some of these particular benefits of mediation are the following:

Private and confidential. Appropriate cases come to the Mediation Center either by the parties themselves or through a referral source. The mediator agrees to keep the contents of the meeting private and confidential; the disputants and the referral source are encouraged to do likewise.

Focus on problem solving, not blame. After the issues of the conflict are explored, the parties are encouraged to talk about their intended behavior in the future, not to dwell on blame and punishment for past behavior.

Simple language. The language of mediation is the everyday language of participants, not the language of someone formally trained in law or another specialized field of study.

Creative solutions. Parties are encouraged to "brainstorm" all possible solutions to their conflict and select the options that make the most sense to them and that they are willing to abide by—many times, the options they select are ones not previously thought of before coming to mediation.

Educational. Skills of good listening, effective summarizing, creative problem solving, and agreement writing are modeled by the mediator and, it is hoped, picked up by the disputants so

I.   SETTING THE STAGE

Mediator's Role: Prepare environment, do introductions, explain ground rules and process.

Participant's Role: Arrive, get settled, agree to ground rules.

II. UNINTERRUPTED TIME

Mediator's Role: Invite first party to talk, then second, manage process.

Participant's Role: Describe conflict and their perception of the issues to mediators, initial expression, and release of emotions around conflict.

III. FOCUSING THE ISSUES

Mediator's Role: Summarize and clarify main issues so that work can begin toward solutions.

Participant's Role: Agree/disagree with summary, clarify main points, surface issues not yet captured by mediator.

IV. THE EXCHANGE

Mediator's Role: Encourage parties to talk, primarily to each other, about their feelings about the issues and their ideas for possible solution. Listen for mediatable issues, points of agreement, set boundaries on topics of discussion, suggest a place to start.

Participant's Role: Respond to issues, accusations, questions from uninterrupted time, fill in information gaps, able to speak freely to other party.

V.   GENERATION OF POTENTIAL SOLUTIONS

Mediator's Role: Summarize mediatable issues, assist in brainstorming of possible options, perhaps hold caucuses to support movement toward agreement or removal of obstacles.

Participant's Role: Accept some responsibility for conflict, suggest some outcomes they would like, explain interests behind positions.

VI. AGREEMENT BUILDING

Mediator's Role: Narrow list of possible solutions, "reality-check" them, assist in negotiation process by parties, capture and write down agreements in specific language that can be agreed to and signed by both parties, make closing statements.

Participant's Role: Negotiate in good faith, not settle for less than one can live with, sign agreement once details have been worked out to parties' satisfaction.

Figure 5.1. A Generic Mediation Process

Source: From *Campus Mediation Center Volunteer Training Manual* by B. Warters. Reprinted by permission of the author.

that they are more likely to engage similar skills in handling differences in the future.

Empowering. The major thrust of mediation is that people get themselves into conflict, and they have the right and responsibility to work their way out of the conflict because they know best what they are willing to commit to and abide by.

Little risk. Evaluation research provides evidence that most cases that come to mediation result in a voluntarily negotiated agreement and the agreements are upheld by the parties. If these conditions do not occur, there are options available for other means of settling the disputes. If mediation does not lead to a mutual agreement, the disputants might be referred to another dispute resolution forum. In the rare cases in which one or more of the disputants do not live up to the agreement, the case can be returned to mediation or handled by some other process.

Mediation has proven to be a useful dispute resolution approach that is gaining significant popularity and success in school systems throughout the nation. It is a powerful strategy that combines knowledge, attitudes, and skills to assist schools in facilitating a more effective learning environment while promoting autonomy and building important life skills for its inhabitants.

Conclusion

In this volume, we have presented five frameworks for preventing or minimizing the escalation of conflict. Agreement management, facilitation, meeting management, consensus decision making, and immediacy are frameworks that, if effectively used, will minimize the likelihood that conflict will emerge in human interaction. In addition, we reviewed mediation as an approach for third parties to help manage conflict once it occurs. The skillful use of these strategies will significantly enhance your confidence and competence in dealing with disputes and differences.

The attitudes, knowledge, and skills developed in all three volumes of our work on conflict resolution are designed to increase the school administrator's resources for constructively managing differences that emerge in the everyday life of the school. In today's demanding and increasingly complex educational environment, administrators are faced with new and difficult challenges. We are confident that the attitudes, knowledge, and skills presented in these books will prove useful in making your efforts successful.

Annotated Bibliography and References

Dana, D. (1989). *Managing differences.* Wolcott, CT: MTI.
A useful "how-to" manual on resolving conflict. Includes a helpful chapter on the uses of mediation in different settings.

Egan, G. (1976). *Interpersonal living: A skills/contact approach to human relations training in groups.* Monterey, CA: Brooks/Cole.
A useful book that presents some important distinctions between processes involved in establishing and keeping rapport and empathy with another. Useful material on use and impact of immediacy skills.

Egan, G., & Cowan, M. A. (1979). *People in systems: A model for development in the human service professions and education.* Monterey, CA: Brooks/Cole.
An interesting work that weaves together innovative thinking on human development and human systems. Offers a particular model and approach to people in systems.

Katz, N. H., & Lawyer, J. W. (1993). *Conflict resolution: Building bridges.* Thousand Oaks, CA: Corwin.
First volume of three-volume set that explores the nature of conflict and its principal sources, helpful attitudes for framing

conflict, and a model and process for resolving conflict in inter-personal and small group settings.

Katz, N. H., & Lawyer, J. W. (1994). *Resolving conflict successfully: Needed knowledge and skills.* Thousand Oaks, CA: Corwin.

Second volume in three-volume series concentrates on core knowledge and skills including establishing rapport and reflective listening, example of a conflict waged and resolved among the authors to illustrate the application of the conflict resolution model and process.

Laborde, G. (1987). *Influencing with integrity: Management skills for communication and negotiation.* Palo Alto: CA: Syntony.

A lively and provocative book that incorporates insights from neurolinguistic programming to enhance the practice of advanced communication and negotiation. Very helpful chapter on making meetings work.

Luft, J. (1984). *Group processes: An introduction to group dynamics.* Mountain View, CA: Mayfield.

One of the most influential works in the literature on group dynamics. Explores laboratory research and basic issues in group process and includes a useful chapter on the teacher and group process.

Steere, D. (Ed.). (1984). *Quaker spirituality: Selected writings.* New York: Paulist.

An anthology of core writings from historical Quaker leaders such as George Fox, Isaac Pennington, John Woolman, Rufus Jones, and Thomas Kelly.

Vroom, V. H., & Yetton, P. W. (1973). *Leadership and decision making.* Pittsburgh: University of Pittsburgh Press.

A classic work that includes informative material on leadership styles, behavior and development, and a widely used model for decision making.

Warters, B. (1992). *Campus mediation center volunteer training manual.* Syracuse, NY: Syracuse University Campus Mediation Center.

A training manual developed and printed by the Campus Mediation Center of Syracuse University.